THE BALLAD OF
THE YORKSHIRE RIPPER

C000068573

BY THE SAME AUTHOR

Poetry
Dark Glasses

Criticism
The Movement: English Poetry and Fiction of the 1950s
Seamus Heaney

As editor, with Andrew Motion
The Penguin Book of Contemporary British Poetry

THE BALLAD OF
THE YORKSHIRE RIPPER
and other poems

BLAKE MORRISON

Chatto *&* Windus LONDON

Published in 1987 by
Chatto & Windus Ltd
30 Bedford Square
London WC1B 3RP

All rights reserved. No part of this publication may
be reproduced, stored in a retrieval system, or
transmitted in any form, or by any means,
electronic, mechanical, photocopying, recording or
otherwise, without the prior permission of
the publisher.

British Library Cataloguing in Publication Data
Morrison, Blake
    The ballad of the Yorkshire Ripper: and other poems.
    I. Title
    821'.914   PR6063.0793/

    ISBN 0-7011-3227-2

Copyright © Blake Morrison 1987

Some of these poems first appeared in the *London Review of Books,
New Statesman,* the *Poetry Book Society Supplement,* 'Poetry Now'
(Radio 3), *Poetry Review, Strawberry Fayre* and the *Times Literary
Supplement.* 'Night Mail' was commissioned by STV for a 1980s'
remake (televised on Channel Four) of the GPO's celebrated thirties'
documentary.

Printed in Great Britain by
Redwood Burn Ltd
Trowbridge, Wiltshire

for my parents

Love wins out but look at all the corpses.
The hero's dais is made of broken bones.
The silence of the dead is not acceptance.
Hearts are dangling like vandalised phones.

The man applauding hasn't been told yet.
Troops are digging where the campion unfurled.
The bride slips her hand inside the bridegroom
As we stretch out on the rack of this tough world.

Contents

Xerox

They come each evening like virgins to a well:
the girls queuing for the Xerox-machine,
braceleted and earmarked, shapely as pitchers
in their stretch Levis or wraparound shirts,
sylphs from the typing pool bearing the forms
of their masters, the chilly boardroom gods.

But this one, this nervous one, is different.
She doesn't gossip with the others and pleads,
when it's her turn, *no, you go first*.
Not until they've gone, their anklets chinking
down the corridor, does she lift the hatch
and dip her trembling hand into the well.

A lightshow begins under the trapdoor:
it flashes and roars, flashes and plashes,
each page the flare of a sabotaged refinery
or the fission of an August storm.
Minutes pass, they slide into the wastebin,
but something is committed for all time.

Sweet-faced, two-faced, a face for every paper,
you were never so alone again.
They took a week or more to find you,
but they found you, posseed to the courtroom
under a scarlet rug, cheeks lit palely
in the lightning of a Nikon swarm.

And what has this to do with it? How you stood
one night by a heifers' drinking-trough
near Yelverton, afraid and down-at-heel
in a mud-churned, midge-drizzling negative,
then saw the country rising from its shadow
under the sudden candour of a moon.

The Kiss

His Buick was too wide and didn't slow,
our wing-mirrors kissing in a Suffolk lane,
no sweat, not worth the exchange of addresses.

High from the rainchecking satellites
our island's like a gun set on a table,
still smoking, waiting to be loaded again.

Spring

That year the year could not get shifting.
Magpies chammered like an engine refusing to fire.
The crocuses were deeply into themselves,
locked in the sooty mantra of their cowls.
No sign of life in the sacs of frogspawn
as they swagged in just-unfrozen ponds.

On the fourteenth of April the bombers left,
a ghost-life of snow slipping from their wings
as the engines warmed, then the desperate sprint
till they lifted with the awkwardness of bustards,
holding a formation like the ten of spades
out across the flatlands to the coast.

And almost at once the field was off –
goosegrass with its hooks getting the hang of things,
brambles laying wire along the backs of hedges,
wafts of bilberry from the orchard,
and up the winding stair of its own making
convolvulus expansive in its cups.

The wheel comes round and the potter pulls up
a stocking of clay. If only we believed
nothing can stop these miracles of burgeoning,
the haws, the umbrils, the ink in the frogspawn,
our kids running for shelter from the paddling pool,
fresh grass mowings velcro'd to their legs.

Shed Load

Like a white drinks tray carried high above the hats
of wedding guests, a hand splayed wide to balance it,
this batch of cow-parsley held itself aloof all summer

but in a week of rain has laid its head down
with the flattened wheat-stems which – puce, sodden –
sprawl in the troughs between freak-swelling waves.

Enough, enough plead the hipless sycamores,
tears running down their wrists, like children
wanting to be hugged and got back on their feet again.

Down the swept coast bedraggled picnics move inside,
a sly porthole cleared in the mist of a windscreen
bringing us this family and news about fish and chips.

And there's nothing to do but watch the valleys shaded
    out,
the blown diagonals like a toddler with a crayon
leaving tracks through a sketchbook's every page.

The whole country shelters in a blackout
where summer should have been, the great stormclouds
with their flares and megaphones keeping us within,

their heavy convoy rumbling in escort through lacy
    hedgerows
which shiver, bow and curtsy at the passing show
of armoury, the wodge of depression,

which moves inside us as we scan the horizon
for a lit crack, a resting-point, a break between lines
or carriages, a stop-off for the driven soul.

On Sizewell Beach

There are four beach huts, numbered 13 to 16,
each with net curtains and a lock.
Who owns them, what happened to the first twelve,
whether there are plans for further building:
there's no one here today to help with such enquiries,
the café closed up for the winter,
no cars or buses in the PAY AND DISPLAY.
The offshore rig is like a titan's diving board.
I've heard the rumours that it's warmer here
for bathing than at any other point along the coast.
Who started them? The same joker who bought
the village pub and named it the Vulcan,
'God of fire and metalwork and hammers,
deformed and buffoonish, a forger of rich thrones'?
Whoever he is, whatever he was up to,
he'd be doused today, like these men out back,
shooting at clay pigeons, the rain in their Adnams beer.
And now a movement on the shingle
that's more than the scissoring of terns:
a fishing boat's landed, three men in yellow waders
guiding it shorewards over metal-ribbed slats
which they lay in front of it like offerings
while the winch in its hut, tense and oily,
hauls at the hook in the prow, the smack with its catch
itself become a catch, though when I lift
the children up to see the lockjaws of sole and whiting
there's nothing in there but oilskin and rope.

I love this place, its going on with life
in the shadow of the slab behind it,
which you almost forget, or might take for a giant's Lego
    set,
so neat are the pipes and the chain-mail fences,

the dinky railway track running off to Leiston,
the pylons like a line of cross-country skiers,
the cooling ponds and turbine halls and reactor control
    rooms
where they prove with geigers on Open Days
('Adults and Children over 14 years only')
that sealed plutonium is less radioactive than a watch.

One rain-glossed Saturday in April
a lad from Halesworth having passed his test
and wanting to impress his girlfriend
came here in the Ford he'd borrowed from his father
and took the corner much too fast, too green to judge
the danger or simply not seeing the child
left on the pavement by the father – no less reckless –
who had crossed back to his Renault for the notebook
he'd stupidly forgotten, the one with jottings
for a poem about nuclear catastrophe,
a poem later abandoned, in place of which
he'd write of the shock of turning round
to find a car had come between him and his daughter,
an eternity of bodywork blotting out the view,
a cloud or an eclipse which hangs before the eyes
and darkens all behind them, clearing at last
to the joy of finding her still standing there,
the three of us spared that other life we dream of
where the worst has already happened
and we are made to dwell forever on its shore.

Proserpina in the Oilfields

I was all right that week in Aberdeen
until the Shell girl brought the tea in
in a Clothkits dress, size 12 not 2,
but the same exactly as Josephine's,
a splaudy web of flowers, its pink-and-blue
smoking out and thinning out my heart
like a rubber glove left too near the gas-ring.

Each day in the abyss of a conference hall
Plundell talked of energy and sunrise,
how Britain – like a sleeper – had rolled over
to the east and this was where the wealth lay,
though I knew from the Olympics of his chain-smoke
that the bottom had dropped out of the ocean
and the fire-breathing rigs would soon expire.

Then the softer touch, that's me, 'a word from personnel'
dispelling the myth of the boorish driller
imprisoned in an underworld offshore,
my brief to the peddlers of real estate,
burger bars, squash clubs and video games
to emphasise his half-year on the mainland
with endless time and money to burn.

Ham off the bone back in the dining room,
each sandstone slice collapsing like a cliff-edge,
and after the bar the rep I'd take up
to my bedroom, his beagle grunts a coming
discreetly or never quite making it,
my legs beyond waving like Jo with nanny
as I commute into the world of men.

Nunhead Motors

A dipping wire of fairy-lights sways
in the wind outside the second-hand lot
as a clattery trade-in pulls up in a blaze
of Simoniz laid on to disguise the daylight
through the bumper, the dents touched up with spray,
and the turning back of the milometer
to an age before the crap in the ashtray
overflowed like a salad of despair.

But at night the frost-skinned cars inside the yard
have the sadness of cattle at a bidding-gate,
blotchy and big-eyed, silent as the guard
dealing hearts to himself over a stove-light,
the low-burning patience of this lot
Everything will work out if we just wait.

Fitter

Measuring tape, monkey wrench, electric saw:
the fitter takes two sugars as before.
From the slack mouth of his canvas tool-bag
brass washers spew like winnings on the floor.

He moans how he's apprenticed for a pittance
because there's nothing else. *Given the chance
I'd start a little business of my own, like.
But to get the loan I need experience.*

I stand like Millais's Christ among the sawdust
taking in his frets – *nice place you've got, must
have cost a bit* – his tongue's serrated edge
flicking between acceptance and mistrust.

Cigarette-end pizzling in the washbowl,
he tightens up his bit to drill a hole –
a bolthole through the newly fixed partition:
Still, mustn't grumble, three million on the dole.

Night Mail

I

Far from the magnets of city and capital,
the pull of money, the gold-stitched runways,
far from all crowds, across the blank pane of the Atlantic,
we come to these islands, the loosened edges of a nation,
their bits and pieces scattered like iron filings,
their hills piled up like slaughtered horses,
their rocky outcrops like jawbones clenched against the
    wind.
Here highland cattle drink from their own shadows,
thistles flaunt their spiky coronets,
and like a splash of blood against the land's anaemia,
a rush and flush of excitement,
spreading the word where words are hoarded,
the red post-van comes threading its way to meet the
    mail-plane,
that pair of scales balancing in the sky,
delicate and clumsy as a dragonfly,
which drops in like a friend each morning,
kissing with its wheels and its hatch of postbags
the upturned face of the earth.

II

After midnight, down the long platforms
spoking outwards from the hub of England,
away from where we lie, coupling and uncoupling,
the unseen industry goes on, the night mail,
work as it sounds still done by men, most of it,
the porters with their mule-packs, the sorters at their boxes
like bees in a hive or doves in a dovecote,
the trolleys skedaddling so that no connection shall be
    missed.
Then the dark shivers under the glare of machines —

planes moving blindly down the empty air lanes,
vans along B-roads lit by cats' eyes and rabbits' eyes,
trains through cuttings of fennel and elderflower –
and like a steamed-up windscreen slowly clearing
we come out in the daze of morning
to this grey milltown lying under a duvet,
its shuttles stopped, its chimneys empty,
a town sleeping in now there's nothing to get up for,
where the streets at dawn used to clatter with the clogs of
    workers
but are hushed now under the tread of the postman,
his bag heavy with nuisance mail and useless mail,
with offers of free films and ads for double glazing,
with fliers for tool hire and come-ons to *Buy us*,
a slagheap of bumf or summonses to pay,
not what they want here, a bond come up,
a job come up, a bigger giro cheque.
Yet still the heart quickens at
the click of the letterflap, the thud on the mat,
all of us hunting the authentic handwritten envelope,
the letters from pen-friends or men friends,
the letters from mothers or brothers or lovers,
and the hope of that makes the postman our favourite
    visitor,
his arm stretching like these trains along embankments,
not juggety-jug now but smooth with self-importance,
like flags or streamers blowing ahead of themselves,
as we ourselves run on towards the future,
its unopened envelope waiting down the line.

Superstore

Sunday, late, at the superstore,
a fresh wind across the car park
plaining through the trolley's mesh,
and doors that slide apart
on a carnival of promo flags,
a vault of infinite shelves.

Baths, tiles, kiddyseats, barbecues,
woodfiller, Polyfilla, turps,
clocks and cassette tapes
separate or in wedlock,
pinewood pews set under smoky tabletops,
rolls of insulation that brings us

round a corner to PRODUCE—
coley and fish fingers,
French loaves and granary loaves,
apples and potatoes laid out
as for Harvest festival
beside a fan of dried-up flowers.

I could go on, and do go on,
past the fly-mos on a prickly strip
of astroturf, the wheel-less wheelbarrows,
the grass seed, weedkiller, lawn feed,
the gnomes fishing lucklessly
in the pre-mould of a pond.

And beyond to the fashion grove,
the aisles of dresses waiting there
like princesses for the awakening touch,
the coat-hangers like Cupid's bows
carried off to screened confessionals
to learn new versions of ourselves.

But that's enough for now: we heave
the trolley to the log-jammed checkout
where girls with singing typewriters
record our losses onto spools
of print-out which they hand us
with an absent smile.

Then out onto the tarmac
past a car boot spilling over
with the corpses of cement bags
and a man and his wife shouting
at each other like Pyramus and Thisbe
through the vents in a louvre door.

And there's not much left of Sunday,
dusk lowering on the roof-racks,
another weekend gone into nothing
as the red-eyed tail-lights
file through the barriered tollgate,
leaving behind the superstore,

its row of lights like the buttons
on a keyboard, its glowing crypts
not a mockery of churches
but a way like them of forgetting
the darkness where no one's serving
and there's nothing to choose from at all.

Him

Like an arctic fox snapping up grounded guillemot chicks
he hangs out in the parks and wastegrounds, the id of
   cities,
for time to bring her to this pretty pass.

Something has broken from the front of his mind
leaving just the back of it, a daubed cave of hunters and
   hunted
where no one but these girls can be allowed.

So he waits for them, leggy like deer in their ankle socks,
loud with an innocence he takes for the lack of it,
full of themselves, full of their mums and dads.

This one especially, wet-eyed as a leveret:
at the corners of sight she flickers like a red ignition light,
coming and going in her striped neck-scarf and PVC mac.

And soon there'll be a day she peels off from the others –
a buckle to be fastened, a brooch to be gone back for –
and then will be the time to introduce himself.

She is the special one who'll grow up in his care,
if she would only stop that screaming, if she could only
be made to understand him, but this is the only way.

Working in lines like beaters at a grouse-shoot,
we go on searching, stony among ferns and bracken,
unable to spring her from his trap.

The Ballad of the Yorkshire Ripper

The 'Red Death' had long devastated the country. No pestilence had ever been so fatal, or so hideous. Blood was its Avatar and its seal . . .
        Edgar Allan Poe, 'The Masque of the Red Death'

I were just cleaning up streets our kid. Just cleaning up streets.
        Peter Sutcliffe to his brother Carl:
  Somebody's Husband, Somebody's Son by Gordon Burn

Ower t'ills o Bingley
stormclouds clap an drain,
like opened blood-black blisters
leakin pus an pain.

Ail teems down like stair-rods,
an swells canals an becks,
an fills up studmarked goalmouths,
an bursts on mind like sex.

Cos sex is like a stormclap,
a swellin in thi cells,
when lightnin arrers through thi
an tha knows there in't owt else.

Ah've felt it in misen, like,
ikin ome part-fresh
ower limestone outcrops
like knuckles white through flesh:

ow men clap down on women
t'old em there for good
an soak up all their softness
an lounder em wi blood.

It's then I think on t'Ripper
an what e did an why,
an ow mi mates ate women,
an ow Pete med em die.

I love em for misen, like,
their skimmerin lips an eyes,
their ankles light as jinnyspins,
their seggy whisps an sighs,

their braided locks like catkins,
an t'curlies glashy black,
the peepin o their linnet tongues,
their way o cheekin back.

An ah look on em as equals.
But mates all say they're not,
that men must have t'owerance
or world will go to rot.

Lad-loupin molls an gadabouts,
fellow-fond an sly,
flappy-skets an drabbletails
oo'll bleed a bloke bone-dry:

that's ow I ear em spoke of
when lads are on their tod,
an ow tha's got to leather em
to stop em gi'in t'nod.

An some o t'same in Bible
where Paul screams fit to bust
ow men are fallen creatures
but womenfolk are t'wust.

Now I reckon this fired Peter,
an men-talk were is goad,
an culprit were our belderin God
an is ancient, bullyin road.

No, Pete weren't drove by vengeance,
rountwistedness or ale,
but to show isen a baufy man –
but let me tell thi tale.

＊

Peter worked in a graveyard,
diggin bone an sod.
From t'grave of a Pole, Zapolski,
e eard – e reckoned – God,

sayin: 'Lad, tha's on a mission,
ah've picked thi out o t'ruck.
Go an rip up prostitutes.
They're nobbut worms an muck.

'Streets are runnin sewers.
Streets are open sores.
Get in there wi thi scalpel
an wipe away all t'oors.'

Pete were pumped like a primus.
E felt is cravin whet.
E started cruisin Chapeltown
but e didn't kill, not yet.

E took a job on t'lorries,
a Transcontinental Ford.
E felt reet good in t'cabin.
E felt like a bloody Lord.

E'd bin a bit of a mardy,
angin on t'old dear's skirt.
E didn't like folks shoutin,
or scraps wi lads, or dirt.

E'd watch his dad trough offal –
trotters, liver, tripe –

or pigeon scraped from t'by-pass,
or rabbit, ung an ripe,

an all e'd felt were babbyish,
a fustilugs, alf-nowt,
an wished e were is younger kid
tekkin lasses out.

But now e'd started truckin
an ropin up is load
an bought isen a Bullworker
e swelled up like a toad,

an stuck is ead in motors
an messed wi carbs an ubs,
an drove wi mates to Manningham
an other arse-end pubs,

or sometimes off to Blackpool
to t'Tower or lights or pier,
or waxworks Chamber of Orrors –
aye, Pete were allus theer.

E met a lass called Sonia,
a nervy type, a shrew,
oo mithered im an nattered,
but Pete, e thought she'd do.

She seemed a cut above im,
a teacher, arty too,
oo wanted summat more'n kids.
Aye, Pete, e thought she'd do.

Cos Sonia, she weren't mucky,
not like yon other bags,
them tarts in fishnet stockins,
them goers, buers, slags.

*

Voice said 'Lad, get crackin:
ah've med thi bombardier.'
Pete blasted red-light districts,
eight lasses in two year.

E slit em up on waste-ground,
in ginnel, plot an park,
in cemetery an woodyard,
an allus after dark.

Is tools were ball-pein ammers,
acksaws an carvin knives,
an a rusty Phillips screwdriver
oned for endin lives.

Cops dint fuss wi fust three,
paid to out on street,
though e blunted blade on is Stanley
deguttin em like meat.

Nor minded marks on fourth lass,
ripped up in her flat,
wi both ends on a clawammer,
split-splat, split-splat, split-splat.

But Jayne MacDonald were a shopgirl
sellin nobbut shoes.
Pete, e killed er anyway
an now e were front page noos.

They appointed a Special Detective,
George Oldfield e were called.
E looked like a country bumpkin,
puffin, red, alf-bald.

E fixed up a Ripper Freefone,
Leeds 5050,
an asked Joe Soap to ring im up
an 'Tell us what you know.'

An folks, they give im names all right:
cousins, neighbours, mates,
blokes what they didn't tek to –
all were candidates.

But Pete, no e weren't rumbled.
E moved to a slap-up ouse,
pebbledash an wi a garden,
an utch to keep is mouse.

Cos Sonia, though she nittered
an med im giddyup,
were potterin too long in t'attic
to mind that owt were up.

An she went so ard at paintin
an scrubbin on ands an knee
she nivver noticed blood on trews
an t'missin cutlery.

*

Two weeks afore they'd folks roun
to drink to movin in
Pete ad topped another lass
an not a soul ad sin.

Now, after tekkin guests ome,
e went to t'mouldy corpse
an slashed it wi a glass pane
an serrated neck wi saws.

E were a one-man abattoir.
E cleavered girls in alves.
E shishkebab'd their pupils.
E bled em dry like calves.

Their napes as soft as foxglove,
the lovely finch-pink pout,
the feather-fern o t'eyelash –
e turned it all to nowt.

Seventh lass e totted
were in Garrads Timberyard.
E posted corpse in a pinestack
like Satan's visitin card.

Eighth were a badly woman
oo'd just come off o t'ward
o Manchester Royal Infirmary
an went back stiff as board.

E id is next on a wastetip
under a sofa's wings.
E stuffed her mouth wi ossair.
Er guts poked through like springs.

An wee Jo Whitaker, just 19,
an Alifax Buildin clerk,
bled from er smashed-egg foread
till t'gutter ran sump-dark.

There were lorry-oil inside er,
an filins in each pore,
which might ave led to Peter
if police ad looked some more.

But Oldfield, e weren't tryin.
E'd ears for nobbut 'Jack':
some oaxer wi a cassette tape
ad sent im reet off track.

Voice on tape were a Geordie's,
a tauntin, growlin loon:
'They nivver learn, George, do they.
Nice chattin. See you soon.'

George fell line an sinker,
a fishook in is pride:
'E thinks e's cock o t'midden
but I'll see that Jack inside.'

Aye, George e took it personal,
a stand-up, man to man,
like a pair o stags wi horns locked
– but Ripper offed an ran,

an wi George left fightin boggarts
e struck again like bleach:
bang in t'middle o Bradford
e wiped out Barbara Leach.

Then Marguerite Walls in Farsley,
strangled wi a noose
(a change from t'usual colander job,
none o t'normal clues).

*

Everyweer in Yorkshire
were a creepin fear an thrill.
At Elland Road fans chanted
'Ripper 12 Police Nil.'

Lasses took up karate,
judo an self-defence,
an jeered at lads in porn shops,
an scrawled stuff in pub Gents,

like: 'Ripper's not a psychopath
but every man in pants.
All you blokes would kill like him
given half a chance.

'Listen to your beer-talk –
"hammer", "poke" and "screw",
"bang" and "score" and "lay" us:
that's what the Ripper does too.'

Aye, e did it again one last time,
to a student, Jacqueline Hill,
in a busy road, wi streetlights,
in a way more twisted still,

blammin er wi is Phillips –
but rest o that ah'll leave,
out o respect to t'family
an cos it meks me eave.

Now cops stepped up on pressure.
George, e got is cards.
Files were took from is ands
an put in Scotland Yard's.

They talked to blokes on lorries
an called at Pete's ouse twice,
but Sonia allus elped im out
wi rock-ard alibis.

It were fluke what finally nabbed im.
E'd parked is car in t'gates
of a private drive in Sheffield
wi ripped off numberplates.

Lass oo e'd got wi im
were known to work this patch.
Cops took em both to t'station
but adn't twigged yet, natch.

Ad e meant to kill er?
E'd brought an ammer an knife
but maundered on alf evenin
ow e cunt stand sight o t'wife.

Then lass passed im a rubber
an come on all coquettish.
But still e didn't touch er.
It were like a sort o death-wish.

E managed to ide is tackle
sayin e wanted a pee.
But later on is ammer
were found by a young PC.

So cops they lobbed im questions
through breakfast, dinner, tea,
till e said: 'All right, you've cracked it.
Ripper, aye, it's me.

'Ah did them thirteen killins.
Them girls live in mi brain,
mindin me o mi evil.
But ah'd do it all again.

'Streets are runnin sewers.
Streets are open sores.
Ah went there wi mi armoury
to wipe away all t'oors.

'Ah were carryin out God's mission.
Ah were followin is commands.
E pumped me like a primus.
Ah were putty in is ands.'

*

This were nub o t'court case:
were Peter reet or mad?
If lawyer could prove im a nutter
e'd not come off as bad.

Were e bats as a bizzum
or t'devil come from ell?
Choice were life in a mental
or a Parkhurst prison cell.

E sat in dock like a gipsy
wi is open sky-blue shirt
an gawped at judge an jury
as if all t'lot were dirt.

Defence called up their experts,
psychiatrists an such,
oo sed Pete weren't no sadist
an didn't rate sex much,

that e'd suffered paranoia,
allucinations too,
an killed cos is mind ad drove im —
so t'gravestone tale were true.

But t'other lot med mincemeat
o those who'd bin Pete's dupe
showin ow e'd outflanked em
to get isen from t'soup.

Cos why, if e were loopy,
ad e allus killed on t'dot,
Friday nights an Saturdays,
in cold blood not in ot?

An why, if e weren't no sadist,
ad e left girls, more 'n once,
wi a hundred stabs in t'breastbone
an planks shoved up their cunts?

An ad he shown repentance
for 't'lasses' or for 't'oors'?
As for t'religious mission:
e'd med it up, of course.

(All through this Pete's bearin
were cold as marble slab,
ard as a joint from t'freezer,
slant as a Scarborough crab.)

Counsels rested cases.
Jury reasoned it through.
Judge said: 'How do you find him?'
'Guilty – ten to two.'

They oiked im off in a wagon
past lynchers urlin abuse
an placards urgin t'government
'BRING BACK CAT AND NOOSE.'

They took im to Parkhurst Prison
to serve is time an more,
an folks said t'other inmates
would know to settle t'score.

But when is face were taloned
wi a broken coffee jar
it weren't for rippin real flesh
but nudes from t'prison *Star*.

An meanwhile rest o t'Sutcliffes
spent up their Fleet Street brass,
an put the boot in Sonia:
'Job's all down to t'lass.

'Our Pete were nivver a nutter.
E'd allus a smile on t'face.
That Sonia nagged im rotten
till e killed oors in er place.

'Cos that's the rub wi women,
they push us blokes too far

till us can't be eld responsible
for bein what us are.'

*

So tha sees, nowt's really altered
though Peter's out o t'way.
Mi mates still booze an charnel.
Weather's same each day.

Ower t'ills up northways
stormclouds thump an drain
like opened blood-black blisters
leakin pus an pain.

An death is like a stormclap,
a frizzlin o thi cells,
a pitchfork through thi arteries,
an tha knows there in't owt else.

It meks me think on Peter,
an what e did an why,
an ow mi mates ate women,
an ow Pete med em die.

Ah love em for misen, like,
their skimmerin lips an eyes,
their ankles light as jinnyspins,
their seggy whisps an sighs,

tiny tarn o t'navel,
chinabowl o t'ead,
steppin cairns o t'backbone,
an all e left for dead.

An I look on em as kindred.
But mates all say they're not,
that men must ave t'owerance
or world will go to rot.

An Pete were nobbut a laikin
o this belderin, umped-up God,
an served is words an logic
to rivet girls to t'sod.

An I don't walk appily out no more
now lasses fear lad's tread,
an mi mates call me a Bessy,
an ah dream of all Pete's dead,

an ow they come again to me,
an we croodle out o eye
in nests o fern an floss-seave
an fillytails in t'sky,

an ah mend em all wi kindness
as we kittle out on t'fells
an learn us t'ease o human love
until there in't owt else.

Moth

This chip of cedarwood
with the linsey-woolsey face
is furred like the ermine
it stole inside one Christmas
while she lay, splay-winged,
beneath my weight.

Our last hunt ball
before the child came!
She'd been a tease that night,
fluttering round Molphey
and the colonel: this curt fuck
was how I paid her back.

Something came, daddy,
something flied into the light
screamed my flu-hot son
half a decade later.
She was God knows where
gallivanting. I couldn't cope.

Orange dots on the back
of a cabbage leaf:
magnified, they are melons,
peardrops, basketweaves,
ribbed like a water-butt
or pocked as a golf ball.

And these become the pupa,
the puppet dolls,
spinning their sex silks
and waggling their tails
towards some chandeliered
apartment of light.

The stuff she came out with!
That tale of a moth kept warm
overnight in her bosom .
then rising at breakfast
from its chrysalis –
I mean, for Christ's sake,

look where it landed us,
balmed and tattered
as this ghost of the wardrobe
which lies in my palm
like her old diary
with marbled covers and spine.

Mates

They are holed up in some bar among the dives
of Deptford, deep in their cups and a packet
of cashew nuts, like Chippy Hackee and cute
little Timmy Tiptoes hiding from their wives.

Any minute now they'll be talking shop
about some crony's record-breaking bender,
like that mate of Terry's banned from his own do
after sinking twenty vodkas and a cop.

Set them up again: I'm holding my tankard
so the cloudy light will set them up –
this mermaid on a forearm, that chinstrap
of a scar – though I'll try not to look hard

for fear of finding myself there, out on the piss
with a black-eyed, sulphurous misogynist.

Pendle Witches

On recs and at swimming pools
we searched for the girl
– shy and uncomeatable –
through whose glimming thigh-tops

the light would make a perfect O,
that florin emptiness
not the token of a virgin
but the hole in a lemmel-stone

to ward off the hags
who ran the Pennines
and who wanted to trap us
in the sossy peat of their maw.

Pomagne

'Be careful not to spill it when it pops.
He'd bloody crucify me if he caught us.'

We had taken months to get to this,
our first kiss a meeting of stalagmite

and stalactite. The slow drip of courtship:
her friend, June, interceding with letters,

the intimate struggle each Friday
under the Plaza's girder of light.

But here we were at last, drinking Pomagne
in her parents' double bed, Christmas Eve

and the last advent-calendar door.
'Did you hear the gate click?' 'No, did you?'

Whinny Moor

Old people will tell you that after death the soul passes over
Whinny-moore, a place full of whins and brambles, and . . .
would be met by an old man carrying a huge bundle of boots; and
if among these could be found a pair which the bare-footed soul
had given away during life, the old man gave them to the soul to
protect its feet whilst crossing the thorny moor.

I was back walking on Lothersdale Moor,
through ling, blackthorn and blips of sheepshit,
over dry-stone walls and up kestrels' airstreams,
back with the becks and original sources,
to land on the fell road under Pinhaw
beside the steamed-up hatchback of a Ford.

The driver's window opened as I stood there.
'Tha'll catch thi death – get in an warm thisen'
said the heathery face, open, bloodshot,
leaning across to unlock the other door.
I limped around and took my seat beside him,
cupping my bones about his leather flask.

That highland nip restored me to the land
of the living and I warmed to my tale:
how I had hiked the backs of the Pennine Way,
leaving at dawn from Todmorden to end –
'down there, see, if this mist would just clear up
a bit' – in the shade of Thornton church.

He glanced, disbelieving, at my plimsolls,
frayed and holy with a flapping sole.
He was a rep for Peter Lord, he said,
nodding behind him at the bootful of boots.
'Ah've worked in shoes near alf a century
an sin all t'flippin lot go reet down'ill.'

Then he asked who I was. 'Morrison, eh,
a name for up ere. I knew thi father well
an t'ole surgery in Water Street.
E did is best by Earby, wi disease an that,
aye an thi mother too, deliverin bairns.
Ad thi no mind to follow in their shoes?

'Ere, ave another swig – tha's like a sheet
what started out as peachy then lost
its colourin in t'wash. Ah tell thi what:
you tek these pumps off me to elp thi ome.
They're seconds, any road, an just your size,
an tha's some sloggin still to Thornton.'

Then I was out beside him shaking hands
as he clattered off across a cattle grid,
turning left down to Elslack by the pines.
He should have come out by the Tempest
but the roak was too mawky to see beyond
the reservoir and he vanished in thin air.

That cardboard box was all I had to show
for our meeting, its pair of char-black pumps
like the ones I'd brought from school for Jeffrey Holmes
the Christmas break after his accident,
the lorry that flicked him from his bicycle
turning my mate into a sickbed ghost.

I laced the eyelets for the journey on
across the bogs and sandylands of moor.
Beside the ink-blot of a rookery
I could make out the nib of Thornton church,
and up behind, like an act of kindness,
a perched, solitary, whitewashed farm.

And in the gorse and peat and heather-scorch
his voice came back again like judgement,
the voice of the tarns with their millstones,

a cairn of slingshot stopping me in my tracks
until the wind brought the grit of a Hargreaves
or one of the Barnoldswick MacBrides:

Get on wi thee, stuck there in t'eather
maunderin and moulderin like a corpse.
What odds would it ave made tha stayin put?
Didst think tha could cure us like thi father?
If tha'd not buggered off at twenty
tha'd as like be a boss at Silentnight,

layin us off wi no brass or future
in this valley of dead vases an mills.
So thank thi lucky stars yon ol divel's
gi'en thi some pumps to get ell out again
an shift thisen sharpish to t'nearest stickle
afore tha's eaten up by t'worms or us.

III

Havens

Come to the window, sweet is the night air!

A brass bedstead, a record still turning,
a pair of empty tumblers in the sink:

while history filled its tanks outside the door
there were always such places to miss it for,

rooms with wine stains and a speckled mirror
unknown alike to the ball-turret gunner

and the captain with his blinding spurs.
If things got out of hand you shut the shutters.

Even the study, the cold spot of the house,
could be warmed and soundproofed by new verse.

Then what's this danger that passes through bricks?
How come we are melting away like this?

Darsham

From here it's only miles to the House in the Clouds,
a madcap water-tower pretending to be home,

and for you a chapter in the same tall story
of the Blythburgh angels and Cromwell's guns.

So these skies press on and turn out to be childhood,
a red tractor on a curved brown field.

We go down to the water and are sand-flies.
We rejoin the lugworm and the celandine.

We listen for cathedral bells at Dunwich
tolling from the graveyards of the sea.

When jets come trailing glory from Lakenheath
you bury your great head between my knees.

Straw-burning

Was it *thrup* or *thrip*,
your word for the thunderflies
that came off the cornfield
with the paddlesteaming combine,
like wafted ashes

clagging to our bodies
and warning us of this:
the yellowing page
set alight at one corner,
the burning of straw.

We can see the flames
rushing towards us
like a lynch-mob,
blood in their eye,
tarring and furring,

until the churn and swirl
of the ploughed field-edge
brings them up short
as a river would
yards from our door.

But deaths come bittily
on the evening wind,
mouse bones and finch skulls,
burnt moths and butterflies,
a wedding from hell.

We take them to bed with us:
our charred dreams
are of a leak at Sizewell
or a Green Giant
razing villages and crops.

This morning they're inside,
these wisps of corn-soot,
making themselves at home,
feathering every windowsill,
shaken out of rugs

like rooks from a rookery
or depositing their tea-leaves
in our mugs.
And the mile-long fires
hanging their sheets

across the bypass
are our summer's cremation,
the last of August
like a loose-leaf notebook
scattered round the globe.

Barn

It is a ruined cowhouse, an out-and-outhouse,
no roof or glass, the cleansed laths like a harp
on which the wind plays out its elegies,
a cattle's come-to come to nothing at all.

Grainy sparrows bathe in the dustbowl
of its forecourt or fly up in the loft,
an attic studio as should be,
all air and space and unobstructed light.

While below, gone to ground under a rafter,
you can see the coffin-blocks of hay,
some still tightly parcelled in their bale-string,
some reseeded with a scalping of grass.

Often, walking past, I've wondered who
the owner was and did he drive the Wolseley
parked out back, thistles in its headlamps
and a mesh of brambles for a rad.

Was he a Tovell or Kett, whose wife ran off
or herd got sick and ruined him,
the weight of which he carried here one morning
and fastened to the roofbeam with a rope?

No, something more banal, plain as this cat
hiding out in a tractor-rut, its fur
blown back like the wheat engrossing it,
as a long gust stirs the mustard slurry

of the rapefields, then skirls towards the air-balloon
floating the logo of a Little Chef,
then off past gleaming shippons and silo-towers,
off through the barracks of a turkey-farm,

off, off, to Lowestoft and Felixstowe,
where homes rise like bread out of breezeblocks
and raw container-ships unload the software
of tomorrow, which I believe in,

or pretend I do, trying not to hear
what these lath songs say about purpose giving out,
how everything fails us but the certainty
of failing, if not now, then in the end.

Cuckoo-pint

A brown matchstick held up in the wind,
the bract-leaf cupped around it like a palm.

March had not extinguished it: there it lurked,
sly as something done behind the sheds,

slithering from its half-unrolled umbrella
as we snipped pussy-willow from the lanes.

To come instead on this old man of the woods,
tanned and cowled and clammed inside his collar,

his shirt-front splattered with tobacco stains,
his poker oozy with tuber-froth,

was like learning by accident a secret
intended for later, exciting

and obscene and not to be gone back on,
like the knowledge of atoms, or death.

Aubade

You'd think from all the fuss
what lies behind the world
was coming to declare itself.

What else can these rooks
be hurrying for, rowing
their skulls towards the light?

Why else these sparrows
squalling round the font
and the pink jumpsuit of a jay?

Nerves are on edge
in the spruce pine.
The milk cannot contain itself.

But when I carry her mug
like a smoking crater
back into the bedroom

there is this sweet mound,
seamed, unbudgeable,
not about to open

to anything like light,
not on your life,
and I slip back inside

to the lamps and downlands
where we are touched
by nothing but ourselves.

Reunion

After months apart to sleep with you again,
not quite the cycle of the comet
we've watched for tonight on the horizon,
but in love's small orbit a dynasty,
an ice age evolving to this moon
of scar tissue underneath your elbow,
the soft freckle galaxy of your cheekbones,
or the rose-pink starburst on your neck.

Did our blood slow to keep us just-alive?
We must have slept the winter out like field mice
or like those birds hauled by a Polish trawler
from the bottom of the Baltic Sea,
deep-frozen bill to bill and wing to wing
but brought to the fireside and reviving.

Ice Age

The heat's on full and our baby's flesh
is pargeted with eczema — flaky whorls
and roseheads, gone over with the oils
lined up here like magi round the crèche.

Fog, ice, Armageddon on the radio.
We can see from the nursery the ghost
of a lorry backed up in its exhaust,
like a polar bear fading into snow.

The trains have stopped running and the drainpipes too —
dried tears everywhere, the Night of the Long Knives,
a set of giant molars in the eaves.

Tusk, tusk, don't cry, mammoth will take care of you:
like stretched accordions the radiators hiss
their nonsense tunes, sealing us with a kiss.

Somebody Loves Us All

I was tired, I suppose, and then hit ice,
no means of steering with the steering wheel,
the car sheering off into the crash rail,
the children waking with synchronised cries —

which is why we are here, in the lit hen-hut
of Motorway Recoveries, Snodland,
where an ESSO-hearted garage-hand
presses through the carbon of our invoice, not

rude exactly but unable to share
the drama of this happening to us,
the wall behind him trophied with photos
of his breakdown truck posed by the remainder

of Maestros and Escorts from which no one
could have passed on to this breathing-space
or heard their name read out into the mouthpiece
of a fingermarked, oil-anointed phone.

Greenstick

Bored, restless, at the end of your tether,
you lay in traction on the children's ward,
flat on back while your arm hung in the balance,
two bone-straightening clock weights dangling down.

I had brought adventures, Captain Hook
and Long John Silver, and read them to you
and to Rupert in the bed across from us,
his leg inside a secret passageway,

who cried all evening for his mum to come,
like Darren, with eczema, whose hands were muffed,
and Rachel (dehydrated) and Adam (broken ribs).
I thought *So this is hell and we are in it*

till I saw while waiting for your X-ray plates
a wheeled man, twenty turning ninety,
as light as you, the stubble on his chin
more or less all that was left of him.

Mist

Remember that old trick mother used to play
on us at Christmas, how she would swathe
in layers of newspaper the necklaces
or bracelet charms she'd bought for us, then sink them
in a box inside another box, etc,
so from thinking she'd given us a dolls' house
we'd be scrabbling through the skins of an onion
unable to find anything at all?

Well, I woke like that today, shawled in the fog
that had draped its fur about the cottage,
buried like a stone inside the tissue
of a jewellery box, a hair in the mohair
of a white Persian, awed but harboured
by petticoats and corset-ribs and underfrills,
as if the goddess of air had let down her skirts
to keep me from the monsters of the earth.

The clock said 7:10. Rising in a daze
I threw a duffel over my nightdress
and plunged through the porch's milky way –
then passed into new clouds of unknowing,
the book I'd stuck my nose in pressing me flat
between its endpapers, fazing and blitzing
till I felt like a finger in the Bible
searching for some marked didactic text.

Through the garden's smoky compartment
I picked my way outward to the road,
where cars drove from the screen they were showing on,
their eyes projectors picking out the spoolmarks
of cats' eyes, their beams roofbeams to crawl along
as they edged through the loft-space, arms held stiffly

to keep them from damage or extinction
under the lowered ceiling, the sunk roof of the world.

Struggling to breathe in all that breathiness,
I retreated to the balmy Aga
and waited for the fog to shuffle off.
But still the powers-that-be would not let be:
stalled drizzle caught in the fuzz of fir trees,
muswebs hung like tents in all the hedges,
and the sky loomed heavy as a wardrobe,
cloudbanks on its swirling walnut door.

Until the sun came down at last round lunchtime,
flaunting its flesh-blaze through negligé,
and I ate by the grille of a window
to witness the garden coming clean.
Only the field beyond would not confess itself,
the shy farmhand walking without legs
to where his tractor stood ticking in clingfoil,
the look of it more distant than the noise.

Layer by layer the mist peeled backward, a tide
retreating till the cottages and trees
that had been sunk beneath it drew up
to their full height. The grass breathed like a steam-bath,
herbed with rosemary and lavender,
drawing me out with a book and deckchair
for a pot of lapsang on the lawn.
I must have nodded off very quickly,

the light behind my eyelids turning sour:
a huge dust-cloud blowing over the rye
was not just carrying dust. Out in the sticks
children's brains curdled in a blizzard of exhaust fumes.
The vapour in the woods changed from fox-breath
and spider-thatch to an acid stripping the pines.

And there were we in the thick of it,
out for a picnic in Rendlesham Woods,

Mummy pouring tea from a thermos
while Daddy took his penknife from the knapsack
to slice apart a gleaming hard-boiled egg.
A single egg, as you and I had been,
but now exploding into hemispheres –
Daddy dead, you gone west, me left behind
with mother, who cried from her barkweave bedspread
to put her from this agony or else.

But when I woke in the morphine of evening
the sky was ridged with quiet like a scallop shell
and a thousand skitterish hedge-sparrows
were flocking in the newly turned-up field.
Sunset through their wings like aluminium,
they sheered off in plinkety fragments
or panicked together like a flapping sail
and swished in one blanket overhead.

Gauzed in muslin, the sun disappeared
way above the place it had been booked for,
soft-landing in rolls of insulation,
and in the dusk the fog crept back again,
stroking my thighs with its erotic tide,
courting me with white delphiniums,
like the night they couldn't get back from London
and left us for the first time by ourselves:

scared and excited we drank Tio Pepe
and pigged a double-decker Milk Tray,
and after, in the sweetpapers that clung
like smoky barnacles to the shagpile,
we played out our drama of abandonment,
Gretel and Gretel hugging each other tight

against the fear we felt, or said we did,
orphans of a pea soup, impossible to part.

How hard from where I am to explain it,
the difference from each other and that night!
Heatwaves and snow come and go like migrants.
Only mist shows that there is always mist,
how even when skies are scorched and see-through
still there's a point beyond the point you've got to,
washy, unfixable, a dead patch on the skin.
It's like starting going to church again,

the heavens boiling unattended
but their powdered air promising me the earth
is just our footstool, that there in the white-lying
fogbanks we shall find the missing lane.
And what we step into, though knowable,
is how we'd always failed to know it,
the air sweet, the brickwork soft against the cheek,
more light from the window than went into it –

or the common with white railings after rain
as two girls with a mud-red retriever
head off from the boredom of the touchline
and re-enter the drive to an estate,
a lion on each gatepost, the sun filtering through
fine as an auriscope, an arcade of limes
opening like a keyhole of eternity
on the grass-seamed cart track to the house.

Notes

'Nunhead Motors': 'A salad of despair'. See Thomas Pynchon's *The Crying of Lot 49* (London: Penguin, 1974), p. 8.

'Night Mail': The poem restores a line which, according to its producer Basil Wright, Auden had to drop from the celebrated documentary of the same title – 'hills piled up like slaughtered horses'.

'The Ballad of the Yorkshire Ripper': For its narrative detail the poem is much indebted to Gordon Burn's excellent study of Peter Sutcliffe, *Somebody's Husband, Somebody's Son* (London: Heinemann, 1984). A second, more oblique account of Sutcliffe, Nicole Ward Jouve's *The Streetcleaner* (London: Marion Boyars, 1986) appeared too late to be a source, though it coincides with the ballad in parts of its analysis. Some of the dialect in the poem was taken from Richard Blakeborough's *Wit, Character, Folklore and Customs of the North Riding of Yorkshire* (1911), which contains a glossary of 4000 words including 'baufy' (strong), 'belder' (to bellow as a bull), 'boggart' (a ghost), 'drabbletail' (an immoral woman), 'fustilugs' (a weak fellow) and 't'owerance' (the upper hand).

'Pendle Witches': On the lemmel-stone, see Blakeborough, op cit, p. 158 and p. 415.

'Whinny Moor': The epigraph comes from Blakeborough, pp. 122–3; the legend also lies behind the anonymous (fifteenth-century?) 'Lyke Wake Dirge'.

'Darsham': The House in the Clouds can be found at Thorpeness, Suffolk.

'Reunion': The birds are described in the 'Digression of Ayre' in Burton, *Anatomy of Melancholy* (1651; 16th edition, 1840), p. 318.